A
SEED
WITH
A
PURPOSE
Katie Stevens

Urban Press
P.O. Box 8881
Pittsburgh, PA 15221-0881
+1.412.646.2780
www.urbanpress.us

One fall morning,
a strong gust of
wind blew
through the trees.

With the wind, a single
seed was taken to a dark,
cold place. The seed
wondered why it was there.
The seed felt very alone.

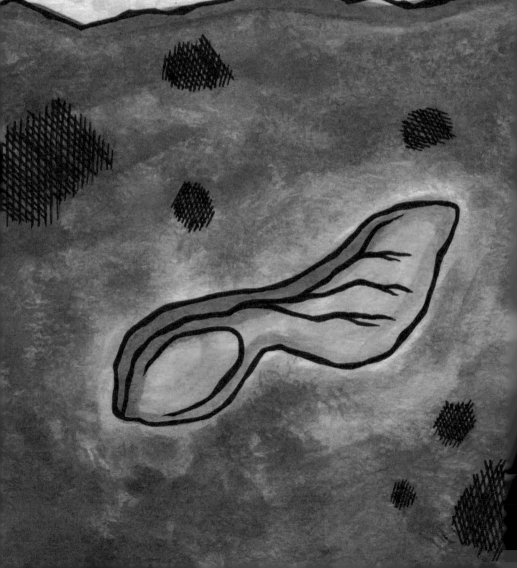

There were days when
the seed felt wet.

There were days when the seed felt hot.

The seed
didn't understand
why this was happening.
This made the seed
very sad.

One day, the seed finally saw daylight! It began to feel strong. Now the seed was a sapling.

But sometimes,
it would get stepped on
and trampled on.

This left the sapling
feeling hurt and broken.

But the
sapling
kept
growing
and
growing
until it
had strong
branches
and a
trunk.
Now it was
a tree!

The tree
swayed in
the wind
and made
shade for
all of the
forest.

The tree
had a
purpose.
And then
the tree
realized...

When it felt very alone in
that dark and cold place,
God placed it there because
He knew it was the best soil.

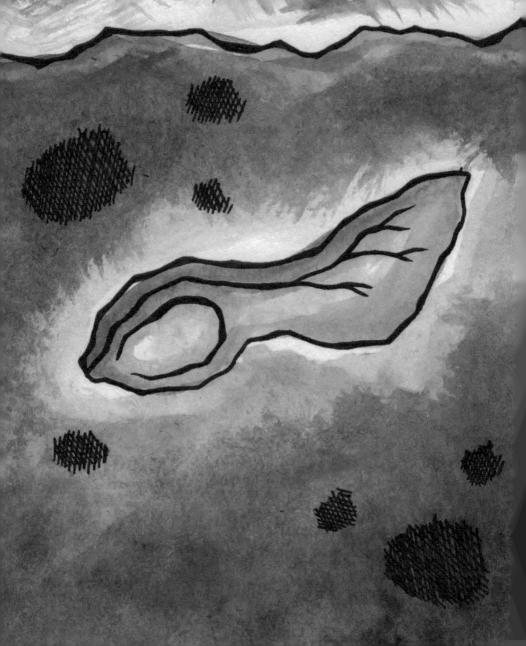

When it felt wet, and hot, and sad, God was using the rain and the sun to allow it to grow.

When it was trampled on and felt hurt and broken, God was making its roots stronger to take hold in that good soil.

It was never alone.
From seed,
to sapling,
to tree,
God had a good
and perfect plan.

And just like the seed, God has a good and perfect plan for you, too.

Made in the USA
Columbia, SC
31 July 2024